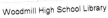

DILEMMA

KT-433-710

CRIME AND PUNISHMENT

PHILIP STEELE

Evans

EVANS BROTHERS LIMITED

First published in 1999 by
Evans Brothers Limited

Evans Brothers Limited
2a Portman Mansions
Chiltern Street
London W1M 1LE

© Evans Brothers Limited 1999

Consultant: Professor David Downes,
Department of Social Policy, London School
of Economics
Editorial: Christopher Westhorp
Design: Tinstar Design (www.tinstar.co.uk)
Production: Jenny Mulvanny

British Library Cataloguing in Publication Data

Steele, Philip
Crime and punishment. – (Moral dilemmas)
1. Criminology - Juvenile literature
I. Title
364

ISBN 0 237 51740 X

ACKNOWLEDGEMENTS

For permission to reproduce copyright material, the author
and publishers gratefully acknowledge the following:

Cover Chris Steele-Perkins/MAGNUM, (central image) Robert Harding, **page 7** Omega/Corbis, **page 8** The Image Works/Topham Picture Point/Timothy Ross, **page 10** Topham Picture Point, **page 13** ET Archive, **page 14** David Lees/©Corbis, **page 17** SIPA/Jeff Vinnick, **page 20** Rex Features/SIPA/David Berwitz, **page 22** Corbis-Bettmann, **page 24** Corbis–Bettmann/UPI, **page 25** SIPA/Rex Features, **page 28** Hulton-Deutsch Collection, **page 30** SIPA/Rex Features, **page 33** Robert Maass/Corbis, **page 35** SIPA/Rex Features, **page 36** Library of Congress/Corbis, **page 39** Rex Features, **page 41** SIPA/Rex Features, **page 42** Corbis-Betmann/Reuters, **page 45** Hulton-Deutsch Collection, **page 47** Topham Picture Point, **page 49** Chris Steele-Perkins/MAGNUM, **page 50** Topham Picture Point, **page 53** Rex Features, **page 55** Wally McNamee/Corbis, **page 56** Underwood & Underwood, **page 57** Topham Picture Point, **page 59** Rex Features

CONTENTS

1. JUSTICE GOES ON TRIAL

Violent crime, murder and social unrest are reported every day on the television news. We see the frightened faces of victims of crime. We see angry crowds facing lines of police, people being arrested and handcuffed, lawyers being interviewed outside courts of law and prisoners protesting in jails.

Newspaper headlines play on our fears: 'THESE GUNS WERE CONFISCATED FROM ELEVEN-YEAR-OLDS – AT SCHOOL' . . . 'AFRAID TO LEAVE THE HOUSE' . . . 'MUGGERS LEAVE TOURIST FOR DEAD'.

Why are crime and punishment always in the news? Firstly, because they really are very important topics. Crime levels indicate whether the society in which we live is functioning properly. Criminal activity can strain the social fabric to breaking point. When that happens we all suffer, even if we are not the direct victims of a crime.

Secondly, by discussing crime and punishment we raise very basic questions about ourselves and about society. We are forced to think about morality and ethics, about what we consider to be right or wrong, fair or unfair. These issues are not abstract. They affect each one of us every day.

When we hear about crime, we begin to wonder how we would react if faced with a similar problem. How would we behave if we were mugged? How would we feel if we were condemned to death? Could we ever report a member of our own family to the police? Would we ever take the law into our own hands? These are personal and often highly emotional matters.

Emotions often get in the way of cool, reasoned debate. Discussing crime and punishment is always difficult. How many of us really know the law or understand how it works? How many of us can agree on how it should work? We may applaud politicians who pledge themselves to fight crime, but how can we find out the real causes of crime when they themselves disagree?

A third reason why we hear so much about crime and punishment might be that sometimes we like to. Some part of us enjoys being shocked, scared, excited, puzzled. We are entertained by television dramas or films which feature the work of the police, law courts, murder and violence.

If we are honest, we have to admit that this may reflect double standards that society has towards criminal activity. We enjoy films in which the bank robbers are shown as daring heroes, but would be furious if our own house was burgled. Sometimes we tend to blame others and make excuses for ourselves. When we are caught speeding, we may complain that the police should be out catching 'real' criminals. In discussing crime and punishment, we should examine our own actions and responsibilities as well as those of other people.

This book looks at how criminal justice systems operate. It raises some questions about the whole confusing issue of crime and punishment. It cannot answer all of them – but it is important for all of us that questions are asked.

In 1995 this face (left) appeared on millions of television screens and newspapers. Former US football star OJ Simpson was accused of murder.

2. WHAT IS A CRIME?

A crime is an act which a government or other authority has declared to be against the law; or it could be a failure to carry out a duty which the law obliges you to fulfil. The stated intention of most legislators, or law-makers, is to protect society and its individual members from harm. Criminal law defines criminal behaviour in detail and may indicate appropriate penalties for each offence. Other branches of law are described on page 16.

The law is enforced by the police, who have the power to arrest and charge those who break it. The offender may be prosecuted by the state, by any other legally empowered authority, or in some cases by a private individual. Judgement and sentencing are carried out by a court of law. A prison service and other agencies ensure that sentences are carried out. This process is sometimes referred to as the penal system.

From murder to mischief

Around the world, many thousands of human acts are deemed to be criminal. They include crimes against the person, such as assault, rape, murder or kidnapping. They include crimes of property or finance, such as burglary, theft or fraud. They include crimes against the state, or against whatever the legislators claim to be the national interest. One example of this might be spying for the enemy during a war.

Crimes may also include making a nuisance of oneself, or threatening, insulting or offending others. They may include the use or sale of certain drugs. They may include all sorts of minor offences, such as parking in the wrong place or dropping litter.

Would there be crimes if there were no laws?

A clash of wills

Crime often represents the collision point between the will of the individual and that of society. The individual wants to do something, but the state forbids it. Crimes may also of course be committed by people acting as a group as well as by lone individuals. For example, a company may be guilty of poisoning rivers with factory waste, or failing to maintain safety on a ferry boat or a train. Public bodies, councils and governments too may commit crimes against the citizens they claim to represent.

Different definitions

So where is the dilemma? Obey the law and you'll have nothing to worry about. Break it, and you'll be punished. Well, perhaps it's not that

Colombian police net a 3-tonne haul of cocaine in August 1994. During the 1970s and 1980s this prohibited drug overtook coffee as Colombia's main export commodity.

simple. Definitions of crime are neither universal nor absolute. This means that they vary greatly from one period of history to another, from one society to another, and from one individual opinion to another.

Laws may even vary greatly within a single nation, from one state or province to the next. The United States of America, Australia and Germany are all examples of federal governments. This means that some of their laws are passed nationally, but others regionally. This may result

Different places. . .
Ideas about what kind of behaviour is criminal and what is not may change greatly over the years. For example, alcohol is classed as an illegal drug in Saudi Arabia, where drinkers of liquor face severe penalties. Alcohol is, however, perfectly legal in the United States of America. This was not always the case: from 1919 to 1933 the manufacture and public consumption of alcohol was banned in America, too. This period, known as the Prohibition Era, saw the rise of illegal trading in liquor by murderous criminal gangs. The anti-alcohol laws created more problems than they solved and so were abolished.

... and different times

Opium is a highly addictive drug made from poppies, which can be processed further to make heroin. Today, opium is strictly illegal in most countries of the world. However, during the 1800s in Europe, opium was used almost as commonly as aspirin is today. China banned opium as early as 1839, but Great Britain, which today is a major enforcer of laws against trafficking in illegal drugs, actually went to war with China twice, in 1840–41 and 1856, in order to force that country to import opium from British-ruled India. In Europe and North America, the change in attitudes towards drugs such as opium dates back to the Hague Convention, an international treaty signed in 1912.

in some confusion or uncertainty for the individual citizen. For example, in some parts of the United States it is illegal to discriminate against homosexuals, while in other places homosexual acts are themselves considered illegal.

Within the United Kingdom, Scotland has a different legal system from that of England and Wales. An invisible political border may be the only reason why a particular activity is labelled as criminal or not.

Governments sometimes pass different laws for different classes of citizen, such as ethnic groups. For example, in South Africa, during the years 1948–94, racist governments passed different laws for their white, black, 'coloured' (mixed race) and Asian citizens. In those days a black person could be committing a crime

Chinese opium addicts in 1880, some forty years after the start of the notorious Opium Wars.

by swimming on a beach where it was perfectly legal for a white person to swim.

Laws are often derived from, or influenced by, differing cultural or religious traditions. Blasphemy – insulting the name of God or a particular set of religious beliefs – may be regarded as a serious crime in most Islamic and some Christian countries, but in others it does not exist at all as a legal offence.

It is not unusual for women of the Bhotia people, who live in parts of Nepal, India and Bhutan, to have more than one husband, while in Saudi Arabia one man may have several wives. The latter practice was at one time also common in the American state of Utah, among people of the Mormon faith. In most countries today, however, the law only permits marriage between one man and one woman.

Do you think there should be just one set of laws for everyone in the world, regardless of where they live? What would be the advantages and disadvantages?

> *There is but one law for all, namely that law which governs all law, the law of our Creator, the law of humanity, justice, equity – the law of nature, and of nations.*
> Edmund Burke, Irish statesman and philosopher (1729–97)

What are laws for?

Laws may vary greatly around the world and over the ages, but the overlap between them has always been far greater than the differences. For example, murder and theft have been outlawed in almost every society since laws have existed.

All kinds of questions arise from this. Is there an absolute, natural justice which overrides the laws made by any one state? Or are laws merely a set of rules, a mechanism to make one particular society function more smoothly? Is the purpose of the law to provide a moral framework for the individual? Or is it to provide an imperfect, but necessary, compromise between the various conflicting interest groups within human society?

> *One law for the Lion and Ox is Oppression.*
> William Blake, English poet and artist (1757–1827)

3. MAKING THE LAW

Could a society function without any laws? It seems unlikely. Take a group of people who live by hunting and gathering wild foods in the remote forests of South America. They may be few in number and face very different problems than people on the crowded streets of New York City. However, they still follow customs and traditions which forbid and punish certain actions. They still need ways of settling their disputes.

It is true, of course, that larger, more complex societies will need many more laws than smaller ones – in much the same way that schools need to have a whole set of binding rules, whereas a single family can manage with a much more informal agreement about, say, the children's bedtime or pocket money.

Who made laws in the past?

Over the ages, laws have been rooted in the various types of society that have developed around the world. There have been feudal societies, based on the ownership of land and the provision of services and food. There have been capitalist societies,

> *This country's planted thick with laws from coast to coast – Man's laws, not God's – and if you cut them down. . . d'you really think you could stand upright in the winds that would blow then?*
> Thomas More in A Man for All Seasons, by English dramatist Robert Bolt, 1960

where most people work for private companies and trade with little government intervention. However, within these societies, such activities have been liable to increasing regulation by the law. There have been communist or socialist societies, where land or businesses are publicly owned and the economy is state-directed.

All these major systems of government have been founded on the rule of law, although this has been operated in very different ways.

Laws are by their nature restrictive, but they are also essential for a free society. Even most anarchists, people who oppose the whole idea of a state, see the need for contracts and agreements between social groups and individuals – while remaining suspicious of the formalities of a court of law.

Laws made by outlaws

Throughout history, small groups of people such as outlaws, runaway slaves or robber bands have chosen to live outside the law, or been forced to do so. But even they have often drawn up strict rules and penalties in order to govern behaviour among themselves. These might include agreements about who could join their gang or whom they should attack. In the 1700s, even pirates signed up to ship's rules, which they disobeyed at their peril. Any pirate caught stealing from another risked being shot, or put ashore on a desert island.

Courts of law, and all the paraphernalia and folly of law. . . cannot be found in a rational state of society. . .
Robert Owen, Welsh social reformer (1771–1858)

Laws written in stone

The drawing up of a legal system or code is often seen as the necessary first step towards a civilised society. Once laws have been written down, it can be ensured that they are clearly understood by all and that they remain the same.

Hammurabi, one of the rulers of the Middle Eastern kingdom of Babylon, drew up a legal code over

3,750 years ago. They dealt mostly with the same kind of practical issues that are discussed in law courts today, such as divorce, inheritance, theft and murder.

The natural law of any society is either tradition (custom) or religion. Any other attempt to draft law for any society, outside these two sources, is invalid and illogical.
Muammar al Qadhafi, Libyan president (1938–)

The law code of Hammurabi; more than 300 of his laws were carved into this block of stone.

Q In ancient Babylon, nobles who broke the law were treated less harshly than the common people. The reverse was true 500 years ago in the North and Central American empire of the Aztecs, where nobles, because of their privileged position in society, were punished more severely. Do you think that was any fairer, or should all classes of people be treated equally before the law?

Many early legal codes were seen as unchanging and eternal truths. They dealt with moral values that could not be questioned. That was because they were based on religious beliefs. The Laws of Moses, dating back to about 1200BC, are a set of moral commands. Jews and Christians believe that these commandments were handed by God to Moses, leader of the ancient Israelites, carved on tablets of stone.

The Hebrew law-giver Moses is said to have received the Ten Commandments from God on Mount Sinai.

Greece and Rome

The ancient Greeks did have legal codes, but they tended not to share the same moral certainties. They saw laws as tools which could be changed or adapted to create a better society. They were the first people to employ professional lawyers.

The basic laws drawn up by the ancient Romans from 450BC onwards were the beginning of a legal system that developed into the great Body of Civil Law drawn up by Emperor Justinian I (c.AD482–565), who ruled the eastern Roman empire from Constantinople (modern Istanbul).

This 'Roman Law' developed over the ages. It gave birth to other bodies of law, such as the code drawn up by France's Emperor Napoleon I in 1804, the Japanese code of 1868 and the German civil code of 1896.

Roman law still has a major influence on many different law systems around the world, including most of Europe.

Common law

'Common law' is a system of law that first grew up in England in the Middle Ages. It was developed by London-based legal authorities called the Inns of Court. Common law was not based on the issuing of royal decrees. In fact it limited the powers of the king and government. Common law evolved instead from the practical decisions made by judges over the centuries. At each trial the judge would consider precedents – previous solutions to similar problems.

Common law spread around the world as the British Empire grew. Today it remains the basis of law in England and Wales, Ireland, most of Canada, the United States, parts of Africa, India, Malaysia, Australia and New Zealand.

Roman and English common law have greatly influenced each other and have become mingled in many countries of the world, such as Scotland and South Africa.

The two major legal traditions have also been influenced by many different local and traditional systems of law, by political structures and by religious teachings or scriptures.

> *To ancient Chinese thinkers such as Confucius (551–479BC), law and order were in themselves a sacred duty. His words of wisdom were: 'What you do not wish done to yourself, do not do to others.' Do you think that might be a good starting point for all law-makers?*

Islamic or Sharia law is practised in many Moslem countries, including Iran, Afghanistan and Sudan. It is based on the teachings of Islam's holy scriptures, the Koran.

From Draco to democracy

Some legal systems in use today are comparatively light or easy. Others are very severe. People often refer to the latter as 'Draconian'. This word comes from the name of an ancient Greek law-maker called Draco. The legal code he drew up for the city-state of Athens in 621BC was so harsh that people later said it had been written in blood. All kinds of petty offences carried the death penalty and anyone who fell into debt could be made a slave. In about 591BC Draco's laws were repealed (overturned) by a more moderate law-maker called Solon. His reforms laid the foundations of the first democracy – in which laws were passed by an elected assembly.

Branches of the law

Just think of all the different reasons for which people go to court. How can anyone make sense of so many possible areas of conflict and dispute? The ancient Romans divided their laws into two main types of procedure – private law and public law.

Most modern laws are divided in much the same way. One-to-one disputes between individuals, groups or corporations are dealt with by private or civil law. Wider issues are dealt with by public law, which may include several branches.

There is constitutional law, which deals with a country's overall legal framework or with the basic rights of its citizens. The US Bill of Rights is one well-known example of a national constitution. It lays out the guiding principles by which the nation is governed, and cannot be as easily overturned or amended as minor laws.

The administrative branch of public law deals with government and the practicalities of running a country. The international branch deals with treaties and agreements between different nations.

Criminal law is that branch of public law which deals with cases of crime and punishment, where the state prosecutes (brings a case against) offenders.

This book mostly discusses criminal law, but of course all the branches of the law are closely linked and often become entangled with one another. For example, if someone is shown to have given false evidence in a civil court, they can be tried for the crime of perjury in a criminal court.

Making laws happen

Any public body which has the authority to make new laws is called a legislature. Today, laws are normally made by national, regional or local governments.

In a democracy, the laws are normally drafted by the government, with the help of legal advisors and members of the civil service (government administrators). They are then brought, sometimes in stages, before a parliament or similar elected assembly for approval, refusal or amendment.

Q *The technology is possible to allow every citizen to vote directly on the passing of every law – but what practical difficulties might have to be faced?*

Direct decisions

Not all laws are decided by representatives in parliaments or assemblies. Sometimes citizens are given a direct vote on a particular issue or problem of the day. This is called a referendum. Referendums are often held to decide on important changes to the constitution. For example, Canada held referendums in 1980 and in 1992 on the constitutional status of the French-speaking Québec province. In American states such as California, law-making decisions called State Propositions may be put directly to voters, by being included on the ballot paper at elections. Each proposition must either be put forward by the state legislature, or else by the public – petitions must have been signed by a sufficient number of voters. Recent propositions in California have raised politically sensitive issues such as bilingual (Spanish-English) education and whether to stop welfare payments to the children of illegal immigrants.

Should Québec province separate from the rest of Canada? Protestors make their point. A referendum brings constitutional law directly to the citizens.

On a raison de dire NON

LA SÉPA RATION?

Some countries have a second layer of government to vet new laws. In Germany there is the Bundesrat ('federal council') and in France the Senate. Such second 'chambers' may be made up of elected representatives, people appointed by the government, religious leaders, regional representatives or traditional figures such as lords or tribal chiefs. Other countries just have single-chamber legislatures, such as the Danish Folketing or the Swedish Riksdag.

Q *Is it a good idea for legislatures to have second chambers to consider new laws? Are they a useful check on badly thought out proposals, or are they just one more layer of bureaucracy? Should they always be elected by the public?*

Responding to the public

In a dictatorship or other tyrannical state, there are no real checks on the law-making process. Laws may simply be issued by the ruler or the governing party as a decree.

As long ago as the days of ancient Greece, political thinkers were already arguing about whether such decrees should be respected as proper laws, or whether they should be seen merely as a form of coercion, as unacceptable tactics by the ruler.

Q *In a democracy, do you have a duty to uphold laws of which you don't approve?*

When push comes to shove
Even democracies may suspend basic laws and rights at times. During a national emergency or a war, special laws may be passed which override the normal constitution or custom. During the conflict in Northern Ireland, laws were passed which allowed alleged terrorists to be detained without a trial. Do you think such laws are sometimes necessary to protect democracy? Or do they weaken democracy by undermining its basic principles?

In most societies, laws are made by a small number of powerful people. That cannot be avoided – legislatures are by their very nature powerful and of limited membership. However, there is always a danger that such groups are not representative and they may, in some cases, abuse their power by making laws which favour their own interests – their social class, perhaps, their political party, or their religion.

> **The good of the people is the supreme law.**
> *Cicero, Roman lawyer and statesman*
> *(106–43BC)*

A democracy should pass laws which are in the interests of the majority of people in society. At the same time it should safeguard the interests of smaller social groups (minorities) and also of individuals. That is a very difficult balance to strike and no legal system can exist that satisfies every individual.

To be just, the law-making machinery must aim to respond to the people as a whole. It must be capable of adapting to the changing needs and structures of society, rather than creating law as a strait-jacket. Legislatures must be prepared to make exceptions to the general rule. For example, under the law of the Aztecs in ancient Mexico, stealing a farmer's crop of maize was a crime punishable by death or slavery. In a land where famine was common, such a harsh penalty was understandable. Hungry travellers, however, were allowed to pick a corn cob from just those rows of plants growing alongside the road. The law was adjusted to take account of reality. In short, laws must be based upon common sense – a consideration which in the common law tradition is called 'equity'. If the laws are stupid or unrealistic, they simply will not work in the long term.

4. BREAKING THE LAW

What kind of people become criminals? Why do people continue to risk all sorts of penalties by breaking the law? In most films or novels, there is little doubt. Some people are heroic and good and some people are just plain bad. For thousands of years, ideas about crime and punishment have been closely linked to such clear-cut notions of morality.

Q *Is being able to choose between good and evil what sets humans apart from the rest of the animal kingdom?*

Mitchell Johnson was just 13 when he was involved in a school shooting in Arkansas. Five people were killed. Who was to blame? Him or his parents? Society at large? Might there have been genetic or psychological causes?

Questions of morality

Definitions of 'good' and 'evil' are often based upon religious teachings or similar cultural traditions. Many non-religious people also choose to use the same terms. In fact most people probably believe that individuals have a choice between good and evil in their daily actions.

Q *If the laws of your religion conflict with the laws of your country, which do you obey?*

20427
364

Good and evil in a religious or moral sense, however, cannot be equated directly with lawful and unlawful behaviour. One would not say that a 50kph speed limit on traffic was in itself good or moral, just that it was safer or more appropriate. And even democratically elected legislatures can pass laws that are unjust.

Even so, morality clearly does play a part in helping us to decide what is criminal or anti-social behaviour. Certainly selfishness and greed seem to lie behind many crimes. In many cases it is fair to say that criminals fail to treat others with the same regard as they have for themselves, or that they put their own interests above those of the rest of society.

Body and mind

Morality apart, can we find other reasons for criminal behaviour? In the 1800s, all kinds of new theories became popular. Some of these falsely claimed to be scientific. In 1808 a German doctor called Franz Joseph Gall published a book called *Functions of the Brain*. He claimed that the shape and formation of each human skull was responsible for the character of its owner. This belief, known as 'phrenology', became very widespread. An Italian criminologist called Cesare Lombroso decided that people of certain physical types were born criminals.

These ideas may seem ridiculous today, and yet it is now claimed that more and more areas of human behaviour may in fact be physically conditioned – by hormones, for example, the chemicals which control the way our body works. When each human being is born, the physical appearance and to some extent the character is 'programmed' by units called genes, based on a chemical known in short as DNA. The genes are inherited from the parents. Although genes may play a part in forming character, it would be scientific nonsense to talk of anyone inheriting a 'criminal gene'. If someone says of a young offender, 'He's a bad one, just like his dad', the problem could stem from parental influence rather than genes.

In modern times, psychology – the scientific study of the mind and how it works – has become a valuable tool in understanding criminal behaviour. It has been shown, for example, that many individuals who have been treated cruelly as children go on to treat children cruelly themselves when they grow up.

> *Violence is, overwhelmingly, an affliction of men rather than women.*
> In the Blood, *by British geneticist Steve Jones, 1996*

An inability to control anger is behind many crimes. A jilted lover may fly into a rage and commit assault or murder – a so-called 'crime of passion'. A car driver may attack another motorist in a fit of 'road rage'.

Psychiatry – the study and treatment of mental illness – also plays an important part in our understanding of criminal behaviour. Many mental illnesses make it very hard for people to fit into society or even to understand the consequences of their actions. People suffering from a series of recognised mental disorders may be urged on to commit acts of violence by imaginary voices in their heads. The medication for many mental illnesses may also make people feel confused and unable to act with due consideration for others.

> **Poverty is the parent of revolution and crime.**
> *Aristotle, Greek philosopher (384–322BC)*

Social causes

Most people now accept that society and environment can be an influence on criminal behaviour. A society which doesn't work properly will breed crime. Many of our ideas about this were first framed by the social reformers and writers of the 1800s, although the idea was already being discussed in ancient Greece thousands of

A cartoon pokes fun at the so-called science of phrenology.

years ago. And of course it does stand to reason that a child who is starving is far more likely to steal a loaf of bread than is a rich, well-fed child.

Economic problems may lie at the root of many crimes. Day after day, advertisements encourage the public to believe that they need expensive trainers, designer clothes, shiny new cars and foreign holidays. Even in the wealthier countries, many people simply cannot afford to buy these things. Small wonder that young people shoplift or go joyriding, say some. Maybe, say others, but can we really absolve individuals from the moral responsibility for their individual actions?

When He told men to love their neighbour, their bellies were full. Nowadays things are different.
From Mother Courage and her Children *(1939)* by German playwright Bertolt Brecht

Particularly in a modern state with welfare systems, is being poor any excuse for stealing?

A moral way to break the law?
Political or economic injustice may turn society into a powder-keg waiting to explode. Riots, violence and widespread crime may result when legitimate grievances are ignored by an undemocratic government. If all peaceful protests fail, are people entitled to resort to violent action?

A moral way forward from this dilemma was proposed by the Indian lawyer and peace campaigner Mohandas Karamchand Gandhi (1869–1948). Campaigning for an end to British rule in India, he openly broke the law and took all the consequences upon himself, including imprisonment. However, he insisted on using non-violent methods of protest, such as marching peacefully or refusing to eat. He called this policy satyagraha, which means 'firmness in truth'. It gave Gandhi and his followers a certain moral authority when they broke the law. Gandhi's campaign was successful, in that India became independent in 1947. Acts of extreme violence were committed by others, however, during his final years and he was himself assassinated.

Q **Should political protest always be within the law? Should it always be non-violent? Would Gandhi's methods have worked against violent dictators such as Adolf Hitler and Idi Amin?**

In 1930, only the Indian government was allowed to produce and tax salt. Gandhi led a march to the sea in violation of the law and collected some salt as a symbolic gesture.

Understanding and prejudice

So who is the true criminal? The individual or society at large? Or is criminality due to a combination of factors? To what extent is it the result of physical, psychological or social conditioning? The truth is often far more complicated than it may seem at first sight, and it is always dangerous to generalise or to condemn criminal behaviour in simplistic terms. Each criminal is an individual and each crime may have its origin in various causes. These must be properly understood if justice is to be served and future crime prevented.

Our perceptions of who breaks the law and who are likely to be the victims of crime often has more to do with prejudice (pre-judgement) than with fact. Who would think, from reading popular newspapers, that young adult males are more likely to be mugged on the street than old ladies? Who would think that a great deal of criminal violence, including half of all murders of women, takes place in the home rather than on the street? Child molesters are more likely to be family friends or relatives than the lone strangers about whom children are so often warned.

Criminals belong to all age groups, all classes, all ethnic groups and both sexes. They are not a separate class of people, but belong to the same society as ourselves. Once certain types of people have been labelled as criminal, however, they often become excluded and ignored by the rest of society. They may be branded by politicians or the press as 'trouble-makers', 'beggars', 'monsters', and so on. This does nothing to help us understand their crimes. Indeed, if people feel they have no connection with the rest of society and if they feel powerless to change things, it may only serve to encourage more criminal activity.

State crimes and the individual

Because criminal law is presented as a confrontation between the state and the individual, it is easy to forget that some of the most sickening crimes ever committed have been organised by the state. The scale of such crimes is hard to take in. More than six million people were murdered by the Nazis during the 1930s and '40s. How were individuals persuaded to gas and burn their fellow human beings? During the Balkan conflict in the 1990s there was also officially

permitted, systematic murder for racist motives. How can such crimes be explained?

Q *Individuals convicted of war crimes often plead that they were only 'obeying orders' from senior army officers or government officials. Is that any kind of excuse?*

Skulls and bones from a mass grave mark the Choeng Ek Memorial in Cambodia. Between 1974 and 1978, during rule by Pol Pot and his Khmer Rouge party, over 3 million Cambodian citizens were killed.

Facts and figures

In order to analyse and properly understand criminal behaviour, people can study statistics for various types of crime. These may show up differences between the social backgrounds of offenders, and between males and females or age groups.

Who offends?

Let's look at one legislature's set of crime figures. The following box lists the type of offences – and who committed them – in England and Wales in 1996. Read through the table and make comparisons between age groups, males/females, and types of offence. Which age

---

Offenders found guilty of, or cautioned for, offences – by gender, type of offence and age: 1996
Source: Home Office, published in Social Trends 1998 Crown copyright

MALES Age	10–13	14–17	18–20	21–34	35 & over	Total
		percentages of total male offenders				no. in 1000s
Theft & handling stolen goods	7	24	16	38	16	153.7
Drug offences	–	12	23	54	1	72.8
Violence against the person	4	22	15	42	17	43.9
Burglary	8	31	20	36	5	40.5
Criminal damage	8	24	16	39	13	11.7
Sexual offences	4	14	7	30	45	6.4
Robbery	6	38	22	30	5	6.0
Other offences	1	8	16	56	19	70.1
All offences	4	20	17	44	15	405.1
FEMALES Age	10–13	14–17	18–20	21–34	35 & over	Total
		percentages of total female offenders				no. in 1000s
Theft & handling stolen goods	10	26	12	34	18	54.5
Drug offences	–	9	18	57	16	8.7
Violence against the person	8	34	10	34	14	7.9
Burglary	15	39	14	25	6	1.8
Criminal damage	7	29	10	37	17	1.2
Sexual offences	10	18	11	32	29	0.1
Robbery	8	51	17	20	4	0.5
Other offences	1	11	15	54	20	11.5
All offences	8	23	13	39	17	86.3

group was charged with the most crime? How do patterns of crime vary between the sexes? Why might more males commit offences than females? Can we learn any lessons from these figures?

> **Pickering: "Have you no morals, man?"**
> **Doolittle: "Can't afford them, Governor. Nor could you if you was as poor as me."**
> *From* Pygmalion *by Irish playwright George Bernard Shaw, 1916*

Comparing crime rates can be very interesting and give a broad picture of the problems facing society and the police. Statistics can be carefully vetted to see if crime rates are falling or rising or if patterns of crime are changing. However, statistics must always be treated with care and it is dangerous to jump to conclusions. Within one country, the figures are at least drawn up in the same way. International comparisons are much more difficult. Countries may have different policies or attitudes towards a particular crime, different detection rates, or different ways of defining or recording crimes.

Crime around the world

Let's take a broader, international viewpoint. Here are some figures for recorded murders, drug offences, robberies and muggings in various countries.
Number of recorded crimes 1994. Source: International Crime Statistics, Interpol

Country	Population	Murders	Robberies, violent thefts	Drug offences
Austria	7,900.000	198	4,615	11,963
Belgium	10,050,000	315	5,659	14,959
Chile	13,440,000	1,545	4,915	3,737
China	1,185,000,000	2,553	not available	38,033
France	57,800,000	2,696	73,310	70,735
Germany	80,800,000	3,751	57,752	132,389
Rep. Ireland	3,600,000	25	2,307	95
Japan	124,900,000	1,279	2,684	23,059
Russian Fed.	150,000,000	32,288	186,450	74,798
Sweden	8,700,000	837	5,331	31,601
USA	257,000,000	23,310	618,820	not available
Zimbabwe	10,700,000	549	10,382	9,109

You can compare these figures in all sorts of ways. Which countries have high rates and which have low ones? What factors might account for the differences? Do countries with high murder rates also have many drug-related offences? What might be the connection? Always remember, the statistics themselves may not compare like to like or be accurate.

5. WHAT KIND OF POLICE?

Who maintains law and order? In Viking Scandinavia or in medieval Ireland, it was often the victim's family or clan who brought the wrongdoer to justice, sought compensation or carried out the execution – in person. Today, in some countries, a private citizen may still make an arrest and hand over the law-breaker to the police.

In later medieval times, each city had 'watchmen', who were often elderly or drunk and no match for criminals. For serious outbreaks of disorder, special forces of troops were raised, or militias of armed private citizens. These often used excessive and illegal force to restore order.

Why do we need police forces?

The first police force was set up in Paris, in 1667, but it was 1829 before policing took on a form we would recognise today. The first police constables in England were the 'Peelers' or 'Bobbies', nicknamed after the politician who founded London's Metropolitan police force,

A political cartoon shows Robert Peel, founder of London's then new police force (1829), having a 'slap at the Charleys' – that is, taking on the old night watchmen.

Sir Robert Peel. In their metal-framed top hats and blue frock-coats, they were often mocked and teased by unruly youths.

Soon police forces were being raised across the world, from Canada's famed North West Mounted Police (the 'Mounties', founded in 1873) to the Victoria Police of Australia, who hunted down the notorious Ned Kelly gang.

> **Ugly, fat-necked, wombat-headed, big-bellied, narrow-hipped, splay-footed. . .**
> Ned Kelly, outlaw, describing the police in Victoria, Australia

Today, it is a fact that every country in the world finds that it needs a professional, properly regulated police force. As society has become more complex, so has criminal activity. The maintenance of law and order can no longer be left to amateurs.

Police duties

The police stand in the front line of the fight against crime, performing a far more complicated and important job than could have been imagined 100 years ago.

Police officers carry out a wide range of duties. They aim to prevent crime from happening in the first place. They investigate crimes that have happened and try to catch criminals and bring them to justice. Police officers are also expected to help the public generally in the case of emergencies or disasters. It is often a dangerous and psychologically distressing job – and a tiring one, too, involving a great deal of patience and long hours of work at all times of the day and night.

Police forces are normally set up by central government, as a federal or national force, or else by region, whether that be a county, state, province, territory or city. Two or more separate levels of policing may exist side-by-side, as in the United States where on a day-to-day basis the police of any one state operate separately from the federal officers.

In many countries, separate police units carry out specialist tasks, such as riot control, traffic duties, public transport policing, criminal investigation, border patrols, drug enforcement or detective work. Many countries have secret police to check on matters of state security.

Across borders

As international communications and travel increase, more and more police work is coordinated between countries. In 1998, English and German police helped their French colleagues identify trouble-makers among the football fans travelling to World Cup matches in France. At that time the countries of the European Union decided to step up cooperation between their forces, forming an organisation called Europol.

Specialist officers of the United States' DEA (Drug Enforcement Administration) have worked closely with local forces in Colombia and Bolivia, the Caribbean and Europe in an attempt to limit the supply of illegal drugs to the USA.

The computers of Interpol (the Lyon-based International Criminal Police Organisation, founded in 1923) help forces track down law-breakers and exchange information worldwide.

Q

Could we or should we have a single world police force?

Special French CRS riot police take a knock as unemployed workers demonstrate outside the Paris Stock Exchange in January 1998.

Serving the public?

Police are normally public servants. Does that mean that they serve the government or the people? There may be a difference. In a democracy, the police are expected to enforce all laws which have been properly passed – whether they personally agree with them or not. If such laws prove to be unpopular, the police may have to face anger on the streets.

If police carry out laws passed by a government, can they be separated from the political process? Can they play an independent role?

There is always a danger that governments will try to use the police in a political role, perhaps for breaking up perfectly legal strikes or protests, or for finding out private or secret information to use against their political opponents. When the communist government of East Germany collapsed in 1989–90, one of the first things people did was to break into the offices of the State Security Police to examine the thousands of secret files they had kept.

Equally, there can be a danger from an independent police force becoming a power in its own right. Many police forces around the world do have democratic controls and checks, of varying effectiveness. Police work may be monitored by publicly appointed committees or authorities.

Some countries have passed laws controlling the amount of information about private citizens held on police files. In many countries, however, the police are hardly neutral, and in some are feared as the brutal agents of dictatorial regimes.

Private police or security guards are used more and more for jobs which were once done by police officers acting as public servants. What problems might such changes of policy create?

There is a burning inside that I have been robbed and I have not got the justice I deserve. . . We have just touched the tip of the iceberg as far as I can see, and we may need other inquiries to look into the cases of the other families.

Neville Lawrence, father of Stephen, murdered in a racist attack, The Guardian, *14 November 1998*

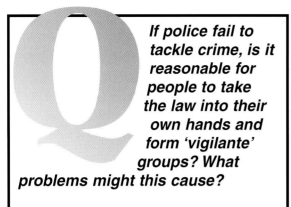

If police fail to tackle crime, is it reasonable for people to take the law into their own hands and form 'vigilante' groups? What problems might this cause?

Zero tolerance?

Even in countries where the police carry out a legitimate role, they face many moral dilemmas in the course of their daily operations. For example, the police have to enforce the letter of the law, but to be successful they may sometimes have to act more subtly and tactfully.

Are there any situations when a police officer should turn a blind eye to a breach of the law? Should minor crimes be ignored if enforcing them might spark off a major breakdown of law and order, such as a riot? Or should police enforce the strategy known as 'zero tolerance', in which they hit any crime, even dropping litter, as hard as they can? In New York City this policy was tried and hailed as a success. Supporters argued that a neighbourhood where petty offences go unchecked becomes more run down and more likely to generate serious crime. Opponents claimed that it raises the pressure in already sensitive areas, or that it simply pushes the problem elsewhere.

Do cops need guns?

Another moral dilemma arises for the police in the question of how much force they should be able to use. Should all police be armed all the time, or – as happens in the United Kingdom – just emergency units, such as those guarding airports and embassies?

Do armed police deter criminals from carrying weapons? There is no evidence from the United States to support that. In fact, arming the police may just raise the stakes. On the other hand, can it be shown that the lack of armed police discourages a gun culture? Attitudes are hard to measure, but the use of firearms has increased dramatically among young city-dwellers in non-armed policing areas of the United Kingdom.

If a criminal is armed, should police officers be entitled to shoot under any circumstances, or only once they have been fired at? Should the offender always be given a verbal warning before shots are exchanged, and a chance to surrender his or her weapon? How can the offender's right to justice compare with the right of a police officer to defend his or her life?

The use of force

Police forces all over the world use many other methods of disabling offenders, from batons and truncheons, to canisters of CS spray, to handcuffs and restraining belts. Crowds may be dispersed with tear gas, powerful water cannon or even plastic bullets. Police officers may also use physical force when arresting someone. These may be less drastic methods than using a firearm, but they still risk injuring or sometimes even killing the alleged offenders.

Most police have strict rules about the use of force, but it is hard to draw up guidelines and anyway rules may be forgotten or ignored in the heat of pursuit or arrest.

Controversial methods

Should it be the job of the police to entrap people – by setting them up to participate in a criminal activity, such as buying illegal drugs, and then arresting them? Is such trickery a fair tactic in the battle against crime? Or is it a distortion of justice? Entrapment may catch a dangerous criminal, but the crime will not have been entirely genuine.

Most police forces use criminals as informers to find out about other criminals. They often reward the informers by protecting them, by not prosecuting them for crimes they are

Gun law, US-style – is it an effective deterrent? Each year, thousands of people are killed with guns in the US.

Q

How much force should the police be allowed to use? Are some methods more acceptable than others?

known to have committed, or by pressing lesser charges than would normally be expected.

Many police operations involve a clash between ideals and compromise. Policing is often a question of deciding which is the lesser of two evils.

Q *Is justice best served by the police letting criminal informers off lightly?*

High-tech or low-tech?

Modern police have the advantages of new technology in dealing with crime. They have fast transport, rapid radio communication and computer information at their fingertips. Is that car stolen? A police patrol can check the registration number as it gives chase down the motorway.

Forensic science – the use of science in criminal investigation and the law – has never been more advanced. Fingerprint experts check the scene of a crime. DNA testing can link a bloodstain to a particular criminal beyond all possible doubt. Psychologists can advise the police on how an individual will act when holding a hostage, or – more controversially – provide a 'profile' of the type of character likely to have committed a certain crime.

All these methods can help solve crimes. However, for some years now there has been a growing realisation that technology can also serve to distance police from the public. A police officer walking a regular beat or patch will probably know what's going on much better than an officer speeding by in a patrol car. Computer information may be valuable, but so is gossip, knowing who is who in the community and what they are up to. Old-fashioned policing methods also have their value in fighting crime.

Q *When a criminal injures a policeman doing his duty they are usually punished more severely. Should corrupt police officers therefore receive harsher sentences?*

Social awareness

To speak of a 'war' against crime is perhaps misleading. Unlike soldiers in battle, the police are acting within the community. They have to do their best to understand it and serve it.

Isolation leads to ignorance and other attitudes which do not help to promote even-handed policing. Justice must be seen to be done publicly.

How many bad apples in a barrel?

Corruption is a serious problem in some police forces around the world, especially where officers are lowly paid and so open to taking bribes. Surely if anyone in society has to be honest, it is the police?

Or do we expect too much of the police force? Aren't its officers subject to just the same pressures as the rest of us? After all, they come from the same society that produces the criminals.

The fact is, there will probably always be police officers who try to live up to the ideals of their profession and there will always be those who are not strong enough to do so. Should it be up to the former to report the latter and to root out any corruption? Or should police work and attitudes be monitored by an independent public authority?

Who should police the police?

A Mafia suspect is brought to justice in Sicily. For many years, this organisation bought off members of the police.

6. A FAIR TRIAL?

In many parts of Europe during the Middle Ages, it was left to God to decide if the accused was guilty. A legal dispute could be settled by a fight to the death or trial by combat – for everyone knew that God would not let an innocent person die. Another popular method was called trial by ordeal. If the accused could, say, lift a stone from a cauldron of boiling water without scalding his hand, then he evidently had God on his side, and was declared innocent.

In the 1600s, suspected witches would be ducked in a river or pond. This type of trial would end in a cruel, catch-all result. If the woman was innocent, she drowned. If she floated to the surface, she obviously had the Devil on her side and was therefore guilty. She would then be taken away and burnt to death. Thousands of innocent women were executed as a result of public hysteria. Similar emotions have often resulted in the public taking the law

Judicial madness: in 1692 the town of Salem, Massachusetts, was in the grip of anti-witchcraft hysteria. Many people were accused of being in league with the Devil.

into their own hands and 'lynching' suspected offenders - murdering them without a formal trial.

Such drastic and superstitious thinking gradually gave way to a much fairer system. Witnesses and accused were still expected to swear before God, but the outcome now depended more on the wisdom of humans, in the form of judges and lawyers.

Who acts as judge?

The people who pass judgement and sentence criminals in a modern court of law make up the judiciary. There may be different ranks of official authorised to judge cases, depending on the seriousness of the offence.

Magistrates or similar officials may form the first line of justice, passing judgement on most minor cases, but referring more serious cases to judges in a higher court. Some of these cases may go on to judges in an appeal court, at which the first verdict is challenged.

A few very important cases might go all the way to a national authority which has the last word on legal decisions. In the United States that is the Supreme Court, in Denmark the Højesteret, and in Britain the House of Lords.

Many European countries have agreed that the European Court of Human Rights, established in 1959, has the right to consider problematic cases from member nations and make obligatory rulings on them.

Judges may be appointed, as in the United Kingdom, or elected by the public, as in the United States. Should they be chosen solely on the grounds of intelligence and experience, or should they reflect the make-up of society as a whole? Should there be more female judges, or more from ethnic minorities?

Does a publicly elected judge have more authority than one who's been appointed? Or is it better for judges to be distanced from any need to seek popularity?

The judge's job

In countries within the common law tradition, such as the USA, Australia or New Zealand, the judge tends to act as a referee between those lawyers acting for the prosecution and those representing the defendant or accused person. However, the judge may interrupt the proceedings in order to ask direct questions.

In countries within the Roman law tradition, such as France, the judge acts more as a public investigator, actively directing the course of the trial in order to reach the truth. Judges may also be empowered to direct criminal investigation outside the courtroom.

Trial by jury

The powers of a judge may be subjected to a kind of democratic control in the form of a jury. This is a body made up of members of the public, which is assigned to the more serious court cases.

The jury considers the facts of the case and decides the verdict (whether the defendant is guilty or not). It is guided in matters of law by the judge who then passes sentence in accordance with the jury's findings.

The jury system has always been popular with the public, but it has its critics in the legal profession. They say that members of the public

Who act as jurors?
Many early medieval legal systems brought in members of the public to assess guilt in criminal cases. The first juries in English common law were really groups of witnesses to the crime, or people of the neighbourhood who knew the defendant or had views on what the verdict should be. Later, the two functions were separated. The lawyers called upon witnesses to give evidence, but the jury was now expected to be unconnected to the case, impartial and independent. Today, defence lawyers may challenge any jurors who they think might be prejudiced against their client.

cannot be expected to make decisions based on very complicated legal questions, even with the direction of a judge. Some say that a jury which has been vetted for the prejudices of its members no longer represents a true cross-section of society. It is also claimed that as many miscarriages of justice have been committed by juries as by judges.

The right to trial by jury, however, has many admirers. Many hold it up as one of the most important freedoms of a democratic society, because it prevents judges becoming tyrannical or out of touch.

The Inquest
If somebody dies in suspicious circumstances, an official called a coroner may call an inquest. This is not a trial at which people can be charged and found guilty or innocent, but witnesses may be called and required to give evidence under oath. It is a public enquiry into the cause of death and may be held before a jury.

The rights of the accused

The notion of what is a fair trial varies greatly around the world. In the more democratic countries, the most basic principle is that the accused is presumed to be innocent until found guilty. He or she cannot be tried twice for the same offence.

Those accused have the right to defend themselves against the charges of the prosecution, or to use a lawyer (an 'advocate') to speak on their behalf. In some legal systems the accused has the right to stay silent without this choice being held against them.

The past criminal record of the accused person is not normally revealed to the court until sentence is passed, or else it may influence the outcome of the trial. Likewise, outside the courtroom the press is forbidden to comment before a verdict is reached. If they do, they may end up in court themselves.

Under the world's more dictatorial legislatures, the accused may have very few legal rights compared with the prosecution. He or she may have no right to a full defence, being allowed only to make a brief statement.

Confessions of guilt may sometimes be forced from the accused by threats or torture. Six hundred years ago, such methods were recognised as a legitimate part of most legal processes. Today they are not, but that doesn't mean the problem isn't still widespread. In 1997 the human rights organisation

War crimes committed in the Bosnian conflict, during the 1990s, highlighted the need for international courts. Here, Dusan Tadic goes on trial in The Hague.

> **What people have always sought is equality before the law.**
> Cicero, Roman lawyer and statesman (106–43BC)

Amnesty International received reports of torture by security forces (police, army or prison officers) from no less than 117 different countries.

> **Ignorance of the law excuses no man: not that all men know the law, but because 'tis an excuse every man will plead, and no man can tell how to refute him.**
>
> John Selden, English politician and historian (1584–1654)

Degrees of guilt

Once the jury or the judge has declared somebody guilty, then surely that is the end of the matter? The accused either committed the crime, or did not. There can be no two ways about it. Of course, it is rarely as simple at that. The notion of guilt is closely linked to ideas about responsibility for one's actions and one's intention to commit a crime. To what extent is a killing accidental or intentional? Is a crime committed in the heat of the moment less severe than one that has been premeditated (carefully worked out beforehand)?

Can young children be held fully responsible for their actions? Not according to most legal systems. But at what age do they understand what is right and wrong? In practical terms, how can that line of responsibility be drawn? Older children may be mature and fully aware of their actions, while some adults may have the mental age and attitudes of a child.

What about the large numbers of crimes committed by people who are insane? If people are not in control of their own mind, can they be held fully responsible? Under most legal systems they cannot, but a judge may still order them to be detained in a psychiatric institution. The trouble is, sanity is very difficult to define. Some people may be only slightly disturbed, some may have periods of clarity followed by periods of confusion or depression.

Questions of motive

The reason for committing a crime is called the motive. To what extent should it determine the degree of guilt or affect the sentence? Is a drunk driver who kills a cyclist less guilty than a murderer? Is someone who blows up a building as a political protest any less guilty than one who does it for personal gain, such as a bank robber? Is someone who helps a chronically ill relative to die really a murderer? Is a girl who has been persuaded to carry drugs through customs more or less guilty than the man who set her up to do it? Are two criminals equally responsible for the same crime, or did one of them lead the other one on?

> *The law is reason, free from passion.*
>
> Aristotle, Greek philosopher
> (384–322BC)

Partners in crime

In October 1994, a young French couple went on a shooting spree, killing three police officers and two taxi-drivers for little apparent motive. The twenty-three-year-old male, Audry Maupin, was killed in the gun battle. His nineteen-year-old girlfriend, Florence Rey, had bought the shotguns which started the trouble and took part in the shootings which followed. But when she came to trial in 1998, she pleaded that she was a vulnerable and weak character who had been under the powerful influence of Maupin. Witnesses, however, described her as a cool killer, who knew just what she was doing. Difficult dilemmas like this one face judges and juries every day. Could the slight, pale and nervous figure of Florence Rey really be a calculating murderess? In this case, said the jury of nine, yes. The judge sentenced her to twenty years in jail.

Florence Rey was convicted by a French jury of murder. Was she any less guilty than her dead boyfriend?

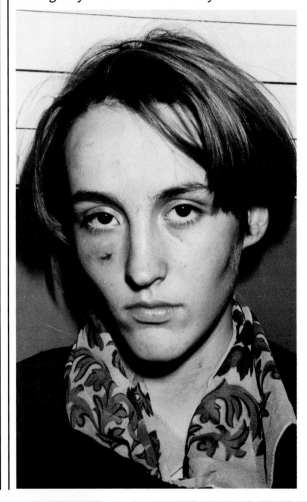

When crime is committed by a group of people or a corporation, how is guilt to be assigned or graded? If an offshore oil rig blows up and kills hundreds of workers, where does the guilt lie?

Reaching a verdict

Judges are in the business of confronting such puzzles and contradictions every day, of taking one person's word against another's. They have to solve these puzzles with a detailed and rational application of the law rather than with emotion or personal judgement.

Judges have to consider the particular aspects of each case in relation to similar cases and judgements that have happened before – to precedents. In common law systems, judges must follow precedents where they exist. In other legal systems, they don't have to – but in practice still often use them as guidelines. Does this make for a legal system which is always looking backwards instead of forwards?

In some courts, as in the United States, a system called 'plea-bargaining' operates. To save the time and money needed to secure conviction for a major crime, the judge will accept a guilty plea to a lesser crime. This may be a practical measure, but does it serve the interests of justice?

Who needs lawyers?

The status and purpose of lawyers in the courtroom varies from one legal system to another. Lawyers are expected to follow the rules which govern their conduct. They don't

In March 1987 some 200 passengers died when a ferry capsized in the North Sea, off Zeebrugge. The ship had sailed with its bow doors open. Who was to blame, the shipping line or the ferry's crew?

have to decide whether their clients are guilty or not, but they must not defend clients as innocent who have privately admitted their guilt.

Lawyers call and cross-examine witnesses and present evidence to the court. This may be direct evidence, such as an eyewitness report of a killing, or circumstantial evidence, such as bloodstains found on an item of clothing. The lawyers end by summing up their case.

The common law system is adversarial rather than investigative. It creates a contest between the prosecution and defence. It relies on the lawyer's skill with words and argument to convince the magistrates or the judge or jury. Hostile witnesses have to be discredited. Is this always the best way in which to get at the truth? Is the outcome often decided by the lawyer's way of presenting the evidence rather than with the essential facts of the case?

As a defence lawyer, would you have a crisis of conscience representing a client you suspected was guilty?

Legal costs

Legal expenses may be huge, so in some countries the state pays legal aid to give less wealthy people access to a professional defence. Since ancient times, lawyers have always been accused of becoming rich at the expense of the client's suffering. One old picture shows two farmers arguing over the ownership of a cow. While one farmer pulls the tail and the other the horns, the lawyer just milks the cow! Do high fees and costs work against a system of fair justice for all? Do they mean there is one law for the rich and another for the poor?

When justice fails

Statues often show the figure of 'Justice' blindfolded – to show that it must be impartial. Some cynics might say that this imagery simply shows 'Justice' failing to see the truth, and miscarriages of justice often do take place even in the world's fairer criminal justice systems: in 1998 a prisoner was released in England after serving twenty-three years in jail – the 'murder victim' had actually died of natural causes.

A fair justice system needs to have effective appeals procedures to review cases. The court of appeal should act as a check on the more dubious decisions of judges and juries, and appeals must be dealt with in an open, honest and painstaking way.

7. FITTING PUNISHMENT?

In 1783 Mary Hughes, a poor woman from Anglesey, in Wales, was found guilty of stealing a nightdress, a waistcoat and a cap. She was sentenced to transportation and shipped off to serve seven years in a penal settlement on the other side of the world – in Tasmania. This voyage alone was a notorious ordeal. A harsh punishment? In those days, you could be hanged for stealing a sheep.

> **And thine eye shalt not pity: but life shall go for life, eye for eye, tooth for tooth, hand for hand, foot for foot.**
> *The Bible: Deuteronomy 19.21*

Hard or soft options?

In the past, penalties for even the most petty crimes were severe. They were often motivated by revenge and designed to inflict the maximum pain and suffering. People were crucified, stoned to death, burned, butchered, tortured, hanged or beheaded.

Deterrents were powerful. Corpses were left on the gibbets at crossroads, as a warning to highwaymen. Imprisonment could mean rotting in a dungeon until death. Public humiliation was common, with people being locked into the pillory or the stocks where the public would laugh at them.

Today's punishments are normally far less severe, although harsh, sometimes brutal, penalties are still enforced in many countries. Do you think that inflicting extreme pain or discomfort should be a thing of the past? Do you think most offenders today are let off lightly? Are most punishments appropriate for the crimes committed?

> **Should punishment be in public, for all to see, or in private? Should it be televised as a warning to others? Or would that just encourage some sick notion of entertainment?**

> **All punishment is mischief: all punishment in itself is evil.**
> *Jeremy Bentham, English writer on ethics and the law (1748–1832)*

> **No State may permit or tolerate torture or other cruel, inhuman or other degrading treatment or punishment.**
>
> *United Nations Declaration Against Torture 1975*

Public enemies – Kabul, 1998

In September 1998 the Islamic religious council or Shura in Afghanistan confirmed the laws which would apply under the country's Taliban government. An example of these laws in action could be seen the following day, when about 10,000 people flocked into a sports stadium in the capital, Kabul, to see justice being done. . . a youth called Atiqullah, convicted of murdering a man during a family argument over water supplies, was shot in the back by his victim's brother. 'It's good', said one spectator. 'We came to see a criminal who deserved to die. We are happy to see such things. . .'

Source: The Guardian 26 September 1998

Why do we punish people?

Just what is the aim of punishing offenders? Is it to enable society to take its revenge? Is it to protect society by preventing them from reoffending? Should the chief purpose of punishment be to deter others from doing the same thing? Is it to rehabilitate offenders by, say, giving them education or job training, so that they can take their place once again in society? Should punishment make offenders see the error of their ways? Or should it be made up of labour which will compensate either society or the victim? All these elements may play a part in deciding penal policy.

Body blows

Corporal (physical) punishment, in the form of beating or flogging, is still common in countries from Saudi Arabia to Pakistan. Many people believe that the pain experienced is corrective, but there is no evidence to suggest that corporal punishment actually achieves such aims. Indeed, it may make the victim less disciplined, more anti-social and violent.

Traditional justice. A man is publicly flogged in a square in Persia (now Iran).

Community pay-back

Some kinds of anti-social behaviour today may be punished by community service orders. The victim may be required to repair a village hall or social club, or help the elderly or disabled. The principle here is that the offender has a debt to repay to society, and will learn from becoming involved in positive action.

When the state prosecutes an offender on behalf of the victim, does it remove an essential personal element from the punishment process? An idea which has proved successful in New Zealand in recent years is for the offenders to meet their victims face-to-face, so as to understand the effects of their crime.

Three strikes and you're out!
In some parts of the United States a policy has been introduced whereby people who receive three convictions – however minor the offences – face life imprisonment. It is a fierce piece of legislation, but is it just? Alternatively, how many chances should society give wrong-doers to mend their ways before it says a line has been crossed?

Hit the pocket

Fines are a common penalty for a wide range of crimes, from traffic offences to public order offences, from tax evasion to fraud. Fines are an effective penalty in many cases, but are often difficult to collect. In many cases they simply can't be met, and this may encourage further criminal activities. On the other hand fines handed out to, say, large corporations found guilty of pollution, may be too small to really hurt.

Should fines be standardised for each offence, or related to the wealth of the offender?

Going to jail

Imprisonment has always been used as a form of punishment. Prisons were once grim hellholes. In the 1800s many countries began to improve living conditions of prisoners, but things remained tough and in many places are still miserable today.

In many countries the number of people sent to jail has increased rapidly in recent years. In the United States, the prison population trebled during the years 1980–98, reaching a high of 1.7 million. It is currently five times higher than the average European figure. In Britain in the early 1990s, prison sentences were actively encouraged by a government which believed that they were an effective method of reducing crime.

In 1996, in the European Union, Portugal had the highest percentage of its population in prison, followed jointly by Spain, Scotland, England and Wales. Greece had the lowest percentage, with Denmark, Finland and Ireland jointly second lowest.

Q *Prisons often try to destroy individualism. Prisoners are given numbers and often have to wear uniforms. Is this fair punishment, or does it just create people who will be unable to function in society when they are released?*

Until recently, these British prisoners had to 'slop out' their own night soil.

Q *Jails provide a single type of punishment in a single place for a wide range of offenders, from murderers to pickpockets, from rapists to drunk drivers. Would it be more effective to have a wider, more appropriate range of punishments and more specialised penal institutions or regimes?*

The vilest deeds, like poison-weeds
Bloom well in prison-air;
It is only what is good in Man
That wastes and withers there.
The Ballad of Reading Gaol, *Oscar Wilde*
(1854–1900)

Who goes to jail? Accused people may be remanded in custody (imprisoned) prior to their trial. Convicted criminals may be sent to jail for anything from a day or two to life, or until their full sentence, say execution, is carried out.

Losing one's freedom for several years is in itself a tough penalty, but losing it for the rest of one's life is a grim ordeal – under whatever conditions.

Many prisoners are released before then for good behaviour. Prisoners who have behaved themselves may be given home leave before being released, but often only if they admit their guilt. This means they may leave jail for an agreed period, provided they promise to return.

Should a criminal's victim be involved in deciding how he or she should be punished?

Prison labour

In some countries, the prison day may be spent in hard labour or in industrial work: in parts of the United States men and women may still be part of a 'chain gang', fettered at the ankle while they work.

In many countries, prisoners may spend the day studying or exercising. In others it may be spent doing nothing, locked in a cell for all or most of the day. Which do you think

---

Prisoners' rights

The European Convention on Human Rights lays out the conditions under which prisoners should be kept. Within member states, prisoners with grievances may take their case to the European Court of Human Rights at Strasbourg. Article 10 declares:

1. All persons deprived of their liberty shall be treated with humanity and with respect for the inherent dignity of the human person.

2. a) Accused persons shall, save in exceptional circumstances, be segregated from convicted persons and shall be subject to separate treatment appropriate to their status as unconvicted persons;

b) Accused juvenile persons shall be separated from adults and brought as speedily as possible for adjudication.

3. The penitentiary system shall comprise treatment of prisoners, the essential aim of which shall be their reform and rehabilitation. Juvenile offenders shall be segregated from adults and be accorded treatment appropriate to their age and legal status.

would be the worst option? Should prisoners be given work to do? If so, should the work be useful to them or to society at large?

A third of those now in prisons should not be there.
Sir David Ramsbotham, UK Chief Inspector of Prisons 1997

Q

> **Should 'life' mean 'life'?**

Q

> **Do prisons act as colleges of crime?**

What kind of prisons?

What is the aim of imprisonment? To punish people by depriving them of their freedom? To remove them from society? To correct or retrain them? There is considerable disagreement and confusion of purpose. Severe punishment or a tough regime may in practice reduce the chance of rehabilitation.

If young people are sent to a prison or young offenders' institution, does it make sense to give them a 'short, sharp shock', including a tough regime of physical exercise, or will that simply make them better qualified to commit further crimes? Should they be trained for a job in the outside world?

Female prisoners in the USA take a break from hard labour on the chain gang.

8. A DEATH FOR A DEATH?

A young woman lies battered to death in the street. She lies in a pool of blood. Her possessions lie scattered around her – letters from her boyfriend, a comb, some photographs. She has been robbed of her money – only enough for a train fare – and a credit card. Her life has been taken, and the lives of her friends and family have been ruined forever. Society has been robbed of great human potential in terms of love and skill and future generations, and all for a few pounds. What punishment is appropriate for her killer? Death?

Of all the debates about crime and punishment, the fiercest of all revolves around capital punishment – execution – which remains the ultimate penalty of the legal system. Capital punishment is normally a sentence for murder, but in some countries it is also a penalty for drug-trafficking, terrorism and various other crimes. In non-democratic countries it is often used to silence political opposition.

The electric chair is still used as a method of execution. It was first employed in the United States in 1890, having first been tried out on animals.

How people are executed

Methods of killing offenders vary around the world, from hanging, shooting, beheading, gassing and electrocution to poisoning or even stoning.

Most methods of execution, such as the notorious guillotine introduced into France in 1791, are chosen for their speed and efficiency. Very few of them, however, do take effect quickly. In 1998 in Guatemala, a prisoner called Martínez Coronado was executed by lethal injection. This was the first time this 'humane' method had been tried in that country. It took him eighteen minutes to die. The execution was broadcast as it took place.

The case for state killing. . .

One of the most common arguments put forward in favour of capital punishment is that it is an effective deterrent, that just the fear of being condemned to death will stop criminals carrying guns. Another common argument is based upon the morality of retribution, and the ancient idea that one death deserves another.

Many societies follow the traditional view that the victim's relations need to avenge their loss. In 1997, when two British nurses were brought to trial in Saudi Arabia for murdering a colleague, the victim's brother, an Australian, was asked if he wished them to be executed. Many victims' families certainly do feel desperate for justice to be done in this way. Is that reasonable, or should they learn to forgive?

The ultimate penalty: facts and figures

– Some 104 countries no longer use the death penalty for crimes such as murder or drug-trafficking, but ninety-one still do.

– Sixty-three countries have abolished the death penalty for all crimes, most recently Belgium, Georgia, Nepal, Poland, Estonia and Azerbaijan.

– In 1997, 2,375 prisoners were executed in forty countries.

– In 1997, 3,707 prisoners were sentenced to death in sixty-nine countries.

– The four countries most likely to execute prisoners are China, Iran, Saudi Arabia and the USA. Between them they carry out 84 per cent of all the world's executions.

– Since 1990, six countries have ignored the UN Convention on the Rights of the Child by executing juveniles (those aged under eighteen): they are Iran, Nigeria, Pakistan, the USA, Yemen and Saudi Arabia.

Source: Amnesty International, 1998

Some people argue on a more practical level. They believe that a quick end is more merciful for the prisoner than a life without hope or purpose, spent in prison. And it is cheaper to execute people, too. Keeping people alive for a lifetime is a very expensive way of spending the taxpayers' money. Capital punishment is claimed to be an effective method of controlling crime. A dead serial killer will never again be able to kill anyone else.

Supporters of capital punishment believe that its opponents often forget the horror of the crime and the grief caused to the victim's family. It is they who deserve society's pity, they say, not the murderer.

> *If the state has the power to send the flower of its manhood to die in thousands for the sake of the lives of the whole community, it would be absurd to deny it the right to put criminals to death if they are a danger to public welfare.*
>
> Heinrich von Treitschke,
> German historian (1834–96)

If you take someone else's life, do you forfeit the right to your own?

. . .and the case against

Critics of capital punishment believe that it fails as a deterrent because most murderers act in a state of desperation. They do not sit down and think rationally about the end result of their action.

How can we know whether or not execution fails as a deterrent? One way would be to see if the number of murders increased in a country such as Canada after 1976, when capital punishment for ordinary crimes was abolished there, and the 'deterrent' effect was removed. No such increase was recorded.

Similarly, there is no hard evidence that capital punishment deters drug-traffickers or indeed people accused of terrorism or treason (attacking the state). Quite the opposite – the latter often become martyrs who inspire the generations to come. After the armed rising in Dublin during Easter 1916, its leaders were caught and executed for treason. The British government believed this would stop the rebels in their tracks.

Instead, the executions shocked so many people in Ireland that it strengthened the struggle against the British and eventually led to Irish independence.

Many critics of capital punishment believe that revenge in itself is immoral. Many religions and philosophies claim that all human life is sacred. They regard execution as just another form of murder, carried out by the state. In the words of the old proverb, two wrongs don't make a right. They also point out that many execution methods in common use are often prolonged and extremely cruel, in effect a form of torture.

> **Research has failed to provide any scientific proof that executions have a greater deterrent than life imprisonment.**
>
> The Death Penalty: A World-wide Perspective
> *by Roger Hood (revised edition 1996)*

Q *Does capital punishment bring the state down to the same level as the murderer?*

No going back

One of the most convincing arguments against capital punishment is that it is the only punishment which is irreversible. Supposing a woman commits a murder and is found guilty. Years later it may be discovered that the police gave false evidence or that the judge's ruling was faulty. It could be that someone else confesses to the murder. If the woman is still serving life imprisonment, she can be released and compensated for the miscarriage of justice. If she has already been sent to the gallows or the electric chair, there can be no final justice.

Derek Bentley, nineteen years old, was hanged after his partner in crime killed an English policeman in 1952. Bentley was posthumously pardoned in 1998.

Evidence can take a very long time to emerge and justice can take a long time to be served. In February 1998 Mahmood Hussein Mattan's conviction for murder in Cardiff, Wales, was overturned – forty-six years after he was hanged.

> **Vengeance is mine;**
> **I will repay, saith**
> **the Lord. . .**
> *The Bible, Romans 12.19*

> **If I were to be murdered. . .**
> **I would not want my life**
> **avenged. Especially by**
> **government – which can't be**
> **trusted to control its own**
> **bureaucrats or collect taxes**
> **equitably or fill a pothole, much**
> **less decide which of its**
> **citizens to kill.**
> *Sister Helen Prejean, American*
> *campaigner against the death penalty*

Death Row, USA

On 17 January 1977 a murderer called Gary Gilmore was shot dead at the Utah State Prison. His execution was the first in the United States for ten years, and it marked the start of a new, widespread use of capital punishment by many of the states – at a time when most other countries around the world were abolishing the death penalty.

By the end of the following twenty years, more than 3,300 American prisoners were awaiting execution. Many had been 'on Death Row' for years, while legal appeals took place and their hopes were raised or dashed.

Over that same two-decade period, 432 people had been executed. They were not always the worst offenders. They were, however, often the poorest and the least educated. That might suggest that it was the prisoners who were not articulate, or wealthy, enough to pay for the best lawyers, who were the ones most likely to be executed. A large percentage were African Americans, which might also suggest that in certain states the judiciary was racist.

> **Judging by past experience, a substantial number of death row inmates are indeed innocent, and there is a high risk that some of them will be executed.**
> US Congress, House Sub-Committee on Civil and Constitutional Rights, 1993

A man tattooed with a crucifix sits on Death Row in the USA. It could be a long wait. Legal appeals can delay executions for many years.

9. CAN CRIME BE BEATEN?

Firefighters try to contain a blaze and prevent the flames from spreading and causing further damage. They then try to put the fire out. The criminal justice system already tries to prevent and contain crime. But can it ever hope to extinguish it once and for all? Will crime always be with us?

The good old days?

Crime has always been with us in the past. For thousands of years, politicians, religious leaders and writers have complained about the unruly youth of their day, about vandalism and lack of respect, about rising levels of crime, about dishonesty and greed. They have often gone on to say that it was never like that in the old days. They look back to some crime-free 'golden age'.

It is much the same today. Some people talk with approval of the 'Victorian values' practised 150 years ago. They forget that there were violent street gangs in Victorian London and that the word 'hooligan' was first used over 100 years ago. Robert Peel, founder of London's police force in 1829, estimated that one in every twenty-two members of the public was engaged in criminal activity at that time. In fighting crime, there is little point in looking back to the 'good old days' for inspiration. Those days never existed.

The good old days? A young angler along the River Thames has a friendly chat with a 'bobby'.

A growing crisis?

It is true that many types of crime have become more common in the last fifty years. Human nature may not have changed, but the problems it faces have. The world is a far more crowded, faster-paced place. People often live under much greater pressure.

Back in the 1800s, the ancient patterns of country life began to break down as people left to seek work in the factories of the growing cities. By the 1990s, many of those great industrial cities had fallen apart too. They no longer had the factories and they had lost their sense of community and neighbourliness.

Housing today is often impersonal. Unemployment is widespread. Films and videos show endless violence and bloodshed. This social environment is potentially explosive and it often just needs a spark to set it off.

Other influences are also commonly blamed for rising crime rates, such as a decline in respect for traditional religious values. Family life too has declined. Grandparents are put into nursing homes, away from family life. Uncles and aunts no longer live in the neighbourhood. Divorce rates rise, single parents struggle to raise children. The social fabric seems to be falling apart.

On the other hand, there is plenty of evidence that in the past religion, rigid family values and a belief in strict discipline themselves gave rise to a great deal of violence and misery. Might our looser society actually function better in some respects than a strait-laced one?

A vicious circle is created as crime makes housing estates derelict and derelict housing estates breed crime. What is the way out? Better designed estates, higher employment or zero tolerance against the vandals?

> **In relation to crime, how can our civilisation be defined? The reply is easy: for thirty years now, state crimes have been far more numerous than individual crimes.**
>
> Albert Camus, French writer, with Arthur Koestler, Hungarian-born writer, in Reflections on the Guillotine (1957)

On a wider scale, the twentieth century has seen world wars, struggles against colonialism, massive social and political disruption. This has given rise to war crimes and state oppression on an unprecedented scale. It has also provided business opportunities for ruthless international criminal organisations such as the Italian Mafia and the Chinese Triads.

Real and imagined problems

Perhaps part of the crime problem in the modern world is one of perception. Crime rates may have risen, but our awareness of crime has risen even more. Crime stories are publicised instantly worldwide through the media. Television brings horrific details of random killings, muggings, hijackings and massacres right into our homes.

People soon become afraid to walk down certain streets or cross the park at night. The elderly begin to fear all groups of noisy young people, even if they are doing no harm. These public fears are like a self-fulfilling prophecy – the empty streets and parks encourage crime and they really do become no-go areas.

Countering crime

So is the battle against crime being lost? What is the best way to tackle it? There are neighbourhood crime prevention schemes. More and more people are put in prison. Technology has brought in all kinds of new methods of pursuing criminals and tackling crime. But is there a danger that we are creating a society which will become a science-fiction nightmare? Will our every move by monitored by cameras on every street corner? Some of these cameras can already be programmed to recognise particular faces. Will we be

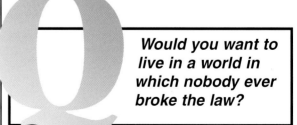

> **Would you want to live in a world in which nobody ever broke the law?**

spied upon by busybody neighbours and secret police?

If so, we are unlikely to defeat crime using solely these methods. More likely, crime will be reduced by wise laws, by police forces which earn the trust of the public, by an honest and realistic judiciary, by consultation with the public, by democratic controls on the possible abuse of power and by a firm but humane penal system. We as individuals have our part to play in creating a less violent, less fearful society by doing our best to respect others and make the community we live in work.

'Big Brother' is watching you. After a series of terrorist attacks, the City of London is now surrounded by a so-called 'ring of steel' with security barriers and closed-circuit TV cameras.

GLOSSARY

adversarial Trial run as a contest.
advocate A lawyer.
blasphemy An insult against God or accepted religious beliefs.
burglary Breaking into a property with the intention of committing a crime.
capital punishment The death penalty; execution of a criminal.
civil law Private law, or a system of law derived from ancient Rome.
code A summary of laws in force.
common law Any system of law derived from medieval England.
compensate To make up for.
constitution The body of legal principles governing a state.
coroner In English law, an official appointed to inquire into the circumstances of a suspicious death.
corporal punishment Punishments to the body, such as flogging.
corrupt Accepting bribes or favours.
crime An act or omission of duty which is prohibited by law.
criminology The scientific study of crime and punishment.
decree A command or order.
defendant The accused person.
deterrence Putting somebody off carrying out a course of action, such as a crime, by fear of punishment.

dictatorship Rule by an unelected leader or government.
equity A sense of fairness or justice.
entrapment The setting up of someone by the police to see if they will commit a crime.
evidence Information presented to a court.
felony A major crime in principle, ranging from theft to murder.
forensic For use by courts of law, particularly relating to science.
coroner In English law, an official appointed to inquire into the circumstances of a suspicious death.
joyriding The driving of a stolen car.
judicial To do with judgement by due process of law.
judiciary That section of the legal system made up of judges and magistrates.
jury A group of members of the public called to decide guilt in a court of law.
legal aid A grant of money to cover legal fees in a court case.
legislator Someone who draws up new laws or revises existing ones.
legislature A body, such as a government, which is authorised to pass new laws.
miscarriage of justice A mistaken

verdict or wrongful penalty.

misdemeanour Any crime that is less serious than a felony.

morality A system of beliefs which approves certain actions as good.

parole A release from jail before the full sentence is completed, conditional upon the prisoner's good behaviour.

perjury Lying under oath to a court.

plea-bargain A compromise struck between judge and defence lawyers.

precedent A legal decision that is used as a model for a later ruling.

prejudice An opinion (often unfavourable) formed before one finds out the truth about something.

premeditate To plan (an action) in advance.

prosecution Carrying out legal proceedings against somebody.

psychiatry The study and medical treatment of mental disorders.

psychology The study of the human mind and how it works.

public law The branch of law which deals with crime and punishment, as well as matters of government and public affairs.

referendum A decision about government policy which is referred directly to the voters.

rehabilitation Preparing a prisoner for return to normal society.

remand prisoner An unconvicted prisoner being held for trial.

repeal To cancel an existing law.

retribution Fitting punishment, given as retaliation for a crime committed.

sentence The penalty ordered by a judge after guilt has been proven.

stocks A wooden framework in which the ankles are locked, formerly used for public humiliation.

terrorism The use of extreme violence to influence a political process, whether by the state or against the state.

treason A crime against the state.

verdict A decision by a judge or jury as to whether someone is guilty or not guilty.

zero tolerance A policy of enforcing all laws, however minor, within a certain area.

INDEX